With love to Marty on
your sixteenth birthday!
Aunt Janet & Uncle Mark

D0031786

Shakespeare's Best

William Shakespeare (1564-1616)

Shakespeare's Best

Memorable Words

From the Great Poems and Plays

With Original Woodcuts

by Don Dubowski

Edited by David Curtis

HALLMARK EDITIONS

CONTENTS

Truth is truth to the end of reckoning.

MEASURE FOR MEASURE   V. I. 45.

There's a time for all things.

COMEDY OF ERRORS   II. II. 66.

*The fire i' the flint shows not
            till it be struck.*

TIMON OF ATHENS   I. I. 22.

*Experience is by industry achieved
And perfected by the swift course of time.*

TWO GENTLEMEN OF VERONA   I. III. 22.

Press not a falling man too far.

KING HENRY VIII,   III. II. 333.

*Be not afraid of greatness: some men are
    born great, some achieve greatness, and
    some have greatness thrust upon them.*

TWELFTH NIGHT   II. V. 156.

They are as sick that surfeit with too much
as they that starve with nothing.

THE MERCHANT OF VENICE   I. II. 5.

The fool doth think he is wise but the wise
man knows himself to be a fool.

AS YOU LIKE IT   V. V. 113.

Good counsellors lack no clients.

MEASURE FOR MEASURE   I. II. 115.

Brevity is the soul of wit.

HAMLET   II. II. 90.

Talkers are no good doers.

KING RICHARD III   I. III. 351.

Often times excusing of a fault
Doth make the fault
the worse by the excuse.

KING JOHN   IV. II. 30.

7

He jests at scars that never felt a wound.

ROMEO AND JULIET   II. II. 1.

Many strokes, though with a little axe,
hew down and fell
the hardest-timbered oak.

KING HENRY VI, PART 3   II. I. 54.

Better a witty fool than a foolish wit.

TWELFTH NIGHT   I. V. 39.

Time shall unfold
what plaited cunning hides.

KING LEAR   I. I. 283.

Our bodies are our gardens, to which
our wills are gardeners.

OTHELLO   I. III. 323.

Friendly counsel cuts off many foes.

KING HENRY VI, PART 1   II. V. 113.

Two may keep counsel
when the third's away.

TITUS ANDRONICUS IV. II. 145.

Naught's had, all's spent,
Where our desire is got without content.

MACBETH III. II. 4.

The devil can cite Scripture for his purpose.

THE MERCHANT OF VENICE I. III. 99.

There is nothing either good or bad
but thinking makes it so.

HAMLET II. II. 259.

Wishes were ever fools.

ANTONY AND CLEOPATRA IV. XV. 37.

There's a place and means
for every man alive.

ALL'S WELL THAT ENDS WELL IV. III. 83.

Sweet mercy is nobility's true badge.

TITUS ANDRONICUS   I. I. 119.

*They that stand high have many blasts
    to shake them.*

KING RICHARD III   I. III. 259.

*Rich gifts wax poor
    when givers prove unkind.*

HAMLET   III. I. 101.

Uneasy lies the head that wears a crown.

KING HENRY IV, PART 2   III. I. 31.

There's small choice in rotten apples.

TAMING OF THE SHREW   I. I. 37.

*One fire drives out one fire; one nail, one
    nail;
Rights by rights falter, strengths by strengths
    do fail.*

CORIOLANUS   IV. VII. 54.

*Better a little chiding than a great deal
of heart break.*

MERRY WIVES OF WINDSOR   V. III. 10.

*The fashion wears out more apparel
than the man.*

MUCH ADO ABOUT NOTHING   III. III. 147.

*The smallest worm will turn,
being trodden upon.*

KING HENRY VI, PART 3   II. II. 17.

Violent fires soon burn themselves out.

KING RICHARD II   II. I. 34.

*Nought so vile that on earth doth live
But to the earth some special good doth give.*

ROMEO AND JULIET   II. III. 17.

Truth will come to light.

THE MERCHANT OF VENICE   II. II. 83.

11

*The robb'd that smiles steals something
from the thief.*

OTHELLO   I. i. 208.

*How oft the sight of means to do ill deeds
Makes ill deeds done!*

KING JOHN   IV. ii. 219.

*Light boats sail swift, though
greater hulks draw deep.*

TROILUS AND CRESSIDA   II. iii. 280.

*A little fire is quickly trodden out;
Which, being suffered, rivers cannot quench.*

KING HENRY VI, PART 3   IV. viii. 7.

Words without thoughts never to heaven go.

HAMLET   III. iii. 97.

Who will not change a raven for a dove?

MIDSUMMER NIGHT'S DREAM   II. ii. 114.

Striving to better, oft we mar what's well.

KING LEAR. I. IV. 369.

Now 'tis the spring, and weeds are
*   shallow-rooted;*
Suffer them now and they'll o'ergrow
*   the garden.*

KING HENRY VI, PART 2   III. I. 31.

He that is stricken blind cannot forget
*   The precious treasure of his eyesight lost.*

ROMEO AND JULIET   I. I. 238.

An honest tale speeds best being plainly told.

KING RICHARD III   I. III. 96.

There is a history in all men's lives.

KING HENRY IV, PART 2   III. I. 80.

Delays have dangerous ends.

KING HENRY VI, PART 1   III. II. 33.

What's in a name? That which we call a rose
By any other name would smell as sweet.

ROMEO AND JULIET   II. II. 43.

Every why hath a wherefore.

COMEDY OF ERRORS   II. II. 45.

Small showers last long,
*   but sudden storms are short.*

KING RICHARD II   II. I. 35.

Great floods have flown from simple sources.

ALL'S WELL THAT ENDS WELL   II. I. 142.

Though patience be a tired mare,
*   yet she will plod.*

KING HENRY V   II. I. 25.

The hardest knife ill-used
*   doth lose his edge.*

SONNET   95

14

Love thyself last: cherish those hearts
   that hate thee;
Corruption wins not more than honesty.
Still in thy right hand carry gentle peace,
To silence envious tongues: be just, and
   fear not,
Let all the ends thou aim'st at be thy
   country's,
Thy Gods, and truth's; then if thou fall'st
   O Cromwell!
Thou fall'st a blessed martyr.

KING HENRY VIII   III. II. 444.

Heat not a furnace for your foe so hot
      That it do singe yourself.

KING HENRY VIII   I. I. 140.

All's well that ends well.

ALL'S WELL THAT ENDS WELL   IV. IV. 35.

One touch of nature makes
      the whole world kin.

TROILUS AND CRESSIDA   III. III. 175.

Beggars mounted run their horse to death.

KING HENRY VI, PART 3   I. IV. 127.

They breathe truth that breathe
*   their words in pain.*

KING RICHARD II   II. II. 8.

We know what we are,
*   but not what we may be.*

HAMLET   IV. V. 43.

We cannot all be masters, nor all masters
*   Cannot be truly followed.*

OTHELLO   I. I. 43.

When I have plucked the rose,
I cannot give it vital growth again.
It needs must wither.
I'll smell it on the tree.

OTHELLO   V. II. 13.

THE VIRTUOUS MAN

How far that little candle throws his beams!
So shines a good deed in a naughty world.

THE MERCHANT OF VENICE   V. I. 90.

Small things make base men proud.

KING HENRY VI, PART 2   IV. I. 106.

Best men are moulded out of faults;
And for the most, become
much more the better
For being a little bad.

MEASURE FOR MEASURE   V. I. 444.

Flattery is the bellows blows up sin.

PERICLES   I. II. 39.

Virtue is bold, and goodness never fearful.

MEASURE FOR MEASURE   III. I. 214.

How apt are the poor to be proud.

TWELFTH NIGHT   III. I. 141.

Men's evil manners live in brass,
              their virtues we write in water.

KING HENRY VIII   IV. II. 45.

Some rise by sin, and some by virtue fall.

MEASURE FOR MEASURE   II. I. 38.

Happy are they that hear the detractions,
    and can put them to mending.

MUCH ADO ABOUT NOTHING   II. III. 248.

Ill deeds are doubled with an evil word.

COMEDY OF ERRORS   III. II. 20.

Virtue itself turns vice, being misapplied;
  And vice sometime's by action dignified.

ROMEO AND JULIET   II. III. 21.

How sharper than a serpent's tongue it is
    To have a thankless child!

KING LEAR   I. IV. 312.

Virtue is beauty.

TWELFTH NIGHT   III. IV. 405.

He lives in fame that died in virtue's cause.

TITUS ANDRONICUS   I. I. 390.

As the sun breaks through the darkest clouds,
So honour peereth in the meanest habit.

TAMING OF THE SHREW   IV. III. 175.

Conceit in weakest bodies strongest works.

HAMLET   III. IV. 114.

'Tis not enough to help the feeble up,
But to support him after.

TIMON OF ATHENS   I. I. 108.

He that filches from me my good name
Robs me of that which not enriches him,
And makes me poor indeed.

OTHELLO   III. III. 155.

Virtue is chok'd with foul ambition.

KING HENRY VI, PART 2   III. I. 143.

Angels are bright still,
        though the brightest fell.

MACBETH   IV. III. 22.

You have lost no reputation at all,
    unless you repute yourself such a loser.

OTHELLO   II. III. 273.

He that is proud eats up himself;
        pride is his own glass,
        his own trumpet, his own chronicle.

TROILUS AND CRESSIDA   II. III. 165.

What stronger breastplate
    than a heart untainted!
Thrice is he armed that has his quarrel just,
And he but naked, though locked up in steel,
Whose conscience with injustice is corrupted.

KING HENRY VI, PART II   III. II. 232.

Wisdom and goodness to the vile seem vile.

KING LEAR   IV. II. 38.

There are no tricks in plain
*   and simple faith.*

JULIUS CAESAR   IV. III. 20.

Love all, trust a few,
Do wrong to none: be able for thine enemy
Rather in power than use,
*   and keep thy friend*
Under thine own life's key:
*   be checked for silence,*
But never taxed for speech.

ALL'S WELL THAT ENDS WELL   I. I. 74.

Assume a virtue, if you have it not.

HAMLET   III. IV. 160.

He was a man, take him for all in all,
*   I shall not look upon his like again.*

HAMLET   I. II. 187.

JOY AND SADNESS

How much better it is to weep at joy
than to joy at weeping.

MUCH ADO ABOUT NOTHING   I. I. 28.

A friend should bear his friend's infirmities.

JULIUS CAESAR   IV. III. 85.

If all the year were playing holidays,
To sport would be tedious as to work.

KING HENRY IV, PART 1   I. II. 226.

Honest plain words best pierce
the ear of grief.

MIDSUMMER NIGHT'S DREAM   V. II. 763.

Patch grief with proverbs.

MUCH ADO ABOUT NOTHING   V. I. 17.

Misery acquaints a man
with strange bedfellows.

THE TEMPEST   II. II. 41.

24

Oft expectation fails, and most oft there
Where most it promises; and oft it hits
Where hope is coldest and despair most fits.

ALL'S WELL THAT ENDS WELL II. I. 145.

Mirth cannot move a soul in agony.

LOVE'S LABOUR'S LOST V. II. 865.

Past and to come seem best,
things present worst.

KING HENRY IV, PART 2 I. III. 108.

Everyone can mask a grief but he that has it.

MUCH ADO ABOUT NOTHING III. II. 28.

The miserable have no other medicine,
but only hope.

MEASURE FOR MEASURE III. I. 2.

A heavy heart bears not a nimble tongue.

MIDSUMMER NIGHT'S DREAM V. II. 747.

A jest's prosperity lies in the ear
Of him that hears it, never in the tongue
Of him that makes it.

LOVE'S LABOUR'S LOST   V. II. 869.

Silence is the perfectest herald of joy:
I were but little happy, if I could
say how much.

MUCH ADO ABOUT NOTHING   II. I. 319.

To weep is to make less the depth of grief.

KING HENRY VI, PART 3   II. I. 85.

I had rather have a fool to make me merry
than experience to make me sad.

AS YOU LIKE IT.   IV. I. 28.

True hope is swift,
and flies with swallows wings;
Kings it makes gods,
and meaner creatures kings.

KING RICHARD III   V. II. 23.

26

Sometimes hath the brightest day a cloud;
And after summer evermore succeeds
Barren winter, with his wrathful
nipping cold:
So cares and joys abound, as seasons fleet.

KING HENRY VI, PART 2   II. IV. 1.

When sorrows come, they come not
as single spies, but in battalions.

HAMLET   IV. IV. 78.

How bitter a thing it is to look into
happiness through another man's eyes.

AS YOU LIKE IT   V. II. 48.

Men can counsel and speak comfort to that
grief which they themselves not feel.

MUCH ADO ABOUT NOTHING   V. I. 20.

Let us not burden our remembrances
With a heaviness that is gone.

THE TEMPEST   V. I. 199.

Small cheer and great welcome
*   makes a merry feast.*

MEASURE FOR MEASURE   III. I. 26.

Give sorrow words; the grief that does not
*   speak*
Whispers the o'er-fraught heart and bids
*   it break.*

MACBETH   IV. III. 209.

Fortune brings in some boats
*   that are not steer'd.*

CYMBELINE   IV. III. 46.

What's gone and what's past help
*   Should be past grief.*

THE WINTER'S TALE   III. II. 223.

ON FEAR AND VALOR

Suspicion always haunts the guilty mind;
  The thief doth fear each bush an officer.

KING HENRY VI, PART 3   V. VI. 11.

Valour is the chiefest virtue,
  and most dignifies the haver.

CORIOLANUS   II. II. 89.

The fear's as bad as falling.

CYMBELINE   III. III. 48.

Fearless minds climb soonest into crowns.

KING HENRY VI, PART 3   IV. VII. 62.

Come what come may
  Time and the hour runs through
    the darkest day.

MACBETH   I. III. 146.

Courage mounteth with occasion.

KING JOHN   II. I. 82.

Cowards die many times before their deaths;
  The valiant never taste of death but once.

JULIUS CAESAR II. II. 32.

The worst is not; so long as we can say
                'this is the worst!'

KING LEAR IV. I. 27.

To fear the foe,
  since fear oppresseth strength,
Gives in your weakness strength
  unto your foe.

KING RICHARD II III. II. 180.

Our doubts are traitors,
And make us lose the good we oft might win,
            By fearing to attempt.

MEASURE FOR MEASURE I. IV. 78.

Care is no cure, but rather corrosive,
  For things that are not to be remedied.

KING HENRY VI, PART 1 III. III. 3.

The better part of valour is discretion.

KING HENRY IV, PART 1   V. IV. 120.

In time we hate that which we often fear.

ANTONY AND CLEOPATRA   I. III. 12.

To be furious
Is to be frighted out of fear,
*   and in that mood*
The dove will peck the hawk.

ANTONY AND CLEOPATRA   III. III. 194.

When valor preys on reason,
*   It eats the sword it fights with.*

ANTONY AND CLEOPATRA   III. III. 199.

In the nights, imagining some fear,
*   How easy is a bush supposed a bear!*

MIDSUMMER NIGHT'S DREAM   V. I. 21.

CONCERNING CONDUCT

O! it is excellent
To have a giant's strength,
            but it is tyrannous
To use it like a giant.

MEASURE FOR MEASURE   II. II. 108.

Give thy thoughts no tongue,
Nor any unproportion'd thought his act.
Be thou familiar, but by no means vulgar;
The friends thou hast, and their
    Adoption tried,
Grapple them to thy soul with
    hoops of steel;
But do not dull thy palm with
    entertainment
Of each new-hatch'd, unfledg'd
    comrade. Beware
Of entrance to a quarrel, but, being in,
Bear't that th' opposed may beware of thee.
Give every man thine ear,
    but few thy voice;
Take each man's censure, but reserve thy
    judgment.
Costly thy habit as thy purse can buy,
But not express'd in fancy; rich, not gaudy;

For the apparel oft proclaims the man,
And they in France of the best
   rank and station
Are most select and generous, chief in that.
Neither a borrower, nor a lender be;
For loan oft loses both itself and friend,
And borrowing dulls the edge of husbandry.
This above all: to thine own self be true,
And it must follow, as the night the day,
Thou canst not then be false to any man.

HAMLET I. III. 59.

Men of few words are the best men.

KING HENRY V III. II. 40.

Be not thy tongue thy own shame's orator.

COMEDY OF ERRORS III. II. 10.

Men should be what they seem.

OTHELLO III. III. 126.

Men's faults do seldom to themselves appear.

THE RAPE OF LUCRECE LINE 633

The time of life is short;
To spend that shortness basely were too long.

KING HENRY IV, PART 1 · V. II. 82.

Few love to hear the sins they love to act.

PERICLES I. I. 92.

Better three hours too soon
than a minute too late.

MERRY WIVES OF WINDSOR II. II. 332.

Mend your speech a little,
Lest you mar your fortunes.

KING LEAR I. I. 96.

Do not give dalliance too much rein.

THE TEMPEST IV. I. 51.

What you cannot as you would achieve,
You must perforce accomplish as you may.

TITUS ANDRONICUS II. I. 106.

There is a tide in the affairs of men,
*   Which, taken at the flood, leads*
*   on to fortune;*
Omitted, all the voyage of their life
*   Is bound in shallows and in miseries.*
On such a full sea are we now afloat;
*   And we must take the current*
*   when it serves,*
*   Or lose our ventures.*

JULIUS CAESAR   IV. III. 217.

Self-love, my liege, is not so vile a sin
*   as self-neglecting.*

KING HENRY V   II. IV. 74.

To do a great right, do a little wrong.

THE MERCHANT OF VENICE   IV. I. 216.

No legacy is so rich as honesty.

ALL'S WELL THAT ENDS WELL   III. V. 13.

Men prize the thing ungain'd more than it is.

TROILUS AND CRESSIDA   I. II. 313.

*Proceed wisely and slow; they stumble
that run fast.*

ROMEO AND JULIET   II. III. 94.

How poor are they that have not patience.

OTHELLO   II. III. 379.

*I charge thee, fling away ambition:
By that sin fell the angels.*

KING HENRY VIII   III. II. 441.

*'Tis a kind of good deed to say well:
And yet words are no deeds.*

KING HENRY VIII   III. II. 153.

*When the lion fawns upon the lamb,
The lamb will never cease to follow him.*

KING HENRY VI   IV. VIII. 49.

ON FINANCE

You pay a great deal too dear
for what's given freely.

THE WINTER'S TALE   I. I. 18.

Our purses shall be proud,
  our garments poor:
For 'tis the mind that makes the body rich.

TAMING OF THE SHREW   IV. III. 173.

Lend less than thou owest.

KING LEAR   I. IV. 133.

He is well paid that is well satisfied.

THE MERCHANT OF VENICE   IV. I. 416.

He that wants money, means, and content
  is without three good friends.

AS YOU LIKE IT.   III. II. 25.

Put money in thy purse.

OTHELLO   I. I. 345.

APPEARANCE AND REALITY

There is some soul of goodness in things evil
Would men observingly distil it out.

KING HENRY V IV. I. 4.

It is a wise father that knows his own child.

THE MERCHANT OF VENICE II. II. 80.

Our remedies oft in ourselves do lie,
Which we do ascribe to Heaven.

ALL'S WELL THAT ENDS WELL I. I. 235.

Have more than thou showest,
Speak less than thou knowest.

KING LEAR I. IV. 133.

Smooth runs the water where
the brook is deep.

KING HENRY VI, PART 2 III. I. 53.

Things sweet to taste
prove in digestion sour.

KING RICHARD II I. III. 236.

The path is smooth that leadeth on to danger.

VENUS AND ADONIS   LINE 788

All that glitters is not gold.

THE MERCHANT OF VENICE   II. VII. 65.

Every cloud engenders not a storm.

KING HENRY VI, PART 3   V. III. 13.

He that is robbed,
  not wanting what was stolen,
Let him not know it,
  and he's not robbed at all.

OTHELLO   III. III. 342.

The fool hath planted in his memory
        An army of good words.

THE MERCHANT OF VENICE   III. V. 71.

When devils will the blackest sins put on,
        They do suggest at first
                with heavenly shows.

OTHELLO   II. III. 357.

There is no vice so simple but assumes
Some mark of virtue on his outward parts.

THE MERCHANT OF VENICE   III. III. 81.

When fortune means to men most good,
She looks upon them with a threatening eye.

KING JOHN   III. IV. 119.

To have what we would have,
we speak not what we mean.

MEASURE FOR MEASURE   II. IV. 117.

What he hath scanted men in hair,
he hath given them in wit.

THE COMEDY OF ERRORS   II. II. 83.

Men judge by the complexion of the sky
The state and inclination of the day.

KING RICHARD II   III. II. 194.

COURTSHIP AND MARRIAGE

Friendship is constant in all other things
Save in the office and affairs of love:
Therefore, all hearts in love use their own
tongues;
Let every eye negotiate for itself,
And trust no agent.

MUCH ADO ABOUT NOTHING   II. I. 184.

Many a good hanging
prevents a bad marriage.

TWELFTH NIGHT   I. V. 20.

Hasty marriage seldom proveth well.

KING HENRY VI, PART 3   IV. I. 18.

That man that hath a tongue, I say, is no man
If with his tongue he cannot win a woman.

TWO GENTLEMEN OF VERONA   III. I. 104.

A young man married
is a man that's marred.

ALL'S WELL THAT ENDS WELL   II. III. 315.

Love moderately; long love doth so;
  Too swift arrives as tardy as too slow.

ROMEO AND JULIET   II. VI. 14.

Trifles light as air
  Are, to the jealous, confirmations strong
      As proofs of holy writ.

OTHELLO   III. III. 323.

'Tis ever common
      That men are merriest
          when they are from home.

KING HENRY V   I. II. 271.

He is the half part of a blessed man,
Left to be finished by such a she;
And she a fair divided excellence,
Whose fulness of perfection lies on him.

KING JOHN   II. I. 437.

A light wife doth make a heavy husband.

THE MERCHANT OF VENICE   V. I. 130.

47

But this swift business
  I must uneasy make, lest too light winning
                Make the prize light.

THE TEMPEST   I. II. 448.

O! beware, my lord, of jealousy;
  It is the green-eyed monster
            which doth mock
                The meat it feeds on.

OTHELLO   III. III. 165.

Look, how my ring encompasseth thy finger,
Even so thy breast encloseth my poor heart;
Wear both of them,
  for both of them are thine.

KING RICHARD III   I. II. 204.

*But, soft! what light through yonder window
breaks?
It is the east, and Juliet is the sun!
Arise, fair sun, and kill the envious moon,
Who is already sick and pale with grief,
That thou her maid art far more fair than she:
Be not her maid, since she is envious;
Her vestal livery is but sick and green,
And none but fools do wear it; cast it off.
It is my lady; O! it is my love:*
        O! that she knew she were.

ROMEO AND JULIET II. II. 2.

*Maids, in modesty, say 'No' to that
Which they would have the profferer
      construe 'Ay.'*

TWO GENTLEMEN OF VERONA I. II. 53.

*Love looks not with the eyes,
    but with the mind.*

MIDSUMMER NIGHT'S DREAM I. I. 234.

Love comforteth like sunshine after rain.

VENUS AND ADONIS LINE 799

Speak low, if you speak love.

MUCH ADO ABOUT NOTHING   II. I. 103.

If ever — as that ever may be near —
You meet in some fresh cheek the power of
fancy,
Then shall you know the wounds invisible
That love's keen arrows make.

AS YOU LIKE IT   III. v. 28.

The course of true love never did run smooth.

MIDSUMMER NIGHT'S DREAM   I. I. 134.

They do not love who show their love.

TWO GENTLEMEN OF VERONA   I. II. 31.

O! they love least that let men
know their love.

TWO GENTLEMEN OF VERONA   I. II. 32.

For love delights in praises.

TWO GENTLEMEN OF VERONA   II. IV. 148.

Beauty itself doth of itself persuade
  The eyes of men without an orator.

THE RAPE OF LUCRECE   LINE 29

Crabbed age and youth cannot live together.
Youth is full of pleasure, age is full of care.

THE PASSIONATE PILGRIM   VERSE XII

Sigh no more, ladies, sigh no more,
  Men were deceivers ever;
One foot in sea and one on shore;
  To one thing constant never.

MUCH ADO ABOUT NOTHING   II. III. 65.

The kiss you take is better than you give.

TROILUS AND CRESSIDA   IV. V. 38.

Beauty provoketh thieves sooner than gold.

AS YOU LIKE IT   I. III. 113.

TO BE OR NOT TO BE

To be, or not to be: that is the question:
Whether 'tis nobler in the mind to suffer
The slings and arrows of outrageous fortune,
Or to take arms against a sea of troubles,
And by opposing end them? To die: to sleep;
No more; and, by a sleep to say we end
The heart-ache and the thousand
    natural shocks
That flesh is heir to, 'tis a consummation
Devoutly to be wish'd. To die, to sleep;
To sleep; perchance to dream:
    ay, there's the rub;
For in that sleep of death what dreams
    may come
When we have shuffled off this mortal coil,
Must give us pause. There's the respect
That makes calamity of so long life;
For who would bear the whips and scorns
    of time,
The oppressor's wrong, the proud man's
    contumely,
The pangs of dispriz'd love, the law's delay,
The insolence of office, and the spurns
That patient merit of the unworthy takes,
When he himself might his quietus make
With a bare bodkin? who would fardels bear,
To grunt and sweat under a weary life,

But that the dread of something after death,
The undiscover'd country from whose bourn
No traveller returns, puzzles the will,
And makes us rather bear those ills we have
Than fly to others that we know not of?
Thus conscience does make cowards of us all;
And thus the native hue of resolution
Is sickled o'er with the pale cast of thought,
And enterprises of great pith and moment
With this regard their currents turn awry,
And lose the name of action.

HAMLET III. I. 56.

All the world's a stage,
And all the men and women merely players:
They have their exits and their entrances;
And one man in his time plays many parts,
His acts being seven ages. At first the infant,
Mewling and puking in the nurse's arms.
And then the whining school-boy, with
    his satchel,
And shining morning face, creeping
    like a snail
Unwillingly to school. And then the lover,
Sighing like furnace, with a woeful ballad
Made to his mistress' eyebrow.

Then a soldier,
Full of strange oaths, and bearded like
    the pard,
Jealous in honour, sudden and quick
    in quarrel,
Seeking the bubble reputation
Even in the cannon's mouth. And
    then the justice,
In fair round belly with good capon lin'd,
With eyes severe, and beard of formal cut,
Full of wise saws and modern instances;
And so he plays his part. The sixth
    age shifts
Into the lean and slipper'd pantaloon,
With spectacles on nose and pouch on side,
His youthful hose well sav'd, a world
    too wide
For his shrunk shank; and his
    big manly voice,
Turning again toward childish treble, pipes
And whistles in his sound. Last scene of all,
That ends this strange eventful history,
Is second childishness and mere oblivion,
Sans teeth, sans eyes, sans taste, sans
    everything.

AS YOU LIKE IT   II. VII. 139.

*Like as the waves make towards the
       pebbled shore,
So do our minutes hasten to their end.*

SONNET 60

*To-morrow, and to-morrow, and to-morrow,
Creeps in this petty pace from day to day,
To the last syllable of recorded time;
And all our yesterdays have lighted fools
The way to dusty death. Out, out,
      brief candle!
Life's but a walking shadow, a poor player
That struts and frets his
      hour upon the stage,
And then is heard no more; it is a tale
Told by an idiot, full of sound and fury,
Signifying nothing.*

MACBETH   V. IV. 19.

*Of all the wonders that I yet have heard,
It seems to me most strange that men
      should fear;
Seeing that death, a necessary end,
Will come when it will come.*

JULIUS CAESAR   II. II. 32.

Just death, kind umpire of men's miseries....

KING HENRY VI, PART 1   II. V. 20.

There's a divinity that shapes our ends,
Rough-hew them how we will.

HAMLET   V. II. 10.

We are such stuff
As dreams are made on, and our little life
Is rounded with a sleep.

THE TEMPEST   IV. I. 156.

The web of our life is of a mingled yard,
good and ill together.

ALL'S WELL THAT ENDS WELL   IV. III. 83.

CHRONOLOGY AND INDEX

Year	*Name of Work*
1590	LOVE'S LABOUR'S LOST: 25, 26
1591	COMEDY OF ERRORS: 6, 14, 19, 35, 44
1591	VENUS AND ADONIS: 43, 50
1592	TWO GENTLEMEN OF VERONA: 6, 46, 50, 51
1592	KING HENRY VI, PART 1: 8, 13, 31
1592	KING HENRY VI, PART 2: 13, 18, 21, 27, 42
1592	KING HENRY VI, PART 3: 8, 11, 12, 16, 26, 30, 38, 43, 46, 58
1593	KING RICHARD III: 7, 10, 13, 26, 31, 48
1593	ROMEO AND JULIET: 8, 11, 13, 14, 19, 37, 47, 50
1593	THE RAPE OF LUCRECE: 35, 52
1594	TITUS ANDRONICUS: 9, 10, 20, 36
1594	KING RICHARD II: 11, 14, 16, 42, 44
1594	MIDSUMMER NIGHT'S DREAM: 12, 24, 25, 32, 50, 51
1594	KING JOHN: 7, 12, 30, 44, 47
1594-99	THE SONNETS: 14, 57
?	THE PASSIONATE PILGRIM: 52
1595	THE MERCHANT OF VENICE: 7, 9, 11, 18, 37, 40, 42, 43, 44, 47
1596	TAMING OF THE SHREW: 10, 20, 40
1597	KING HENRY IV, PART 1: 24, 32, 36
1598	KING HENRY IV, PART 2: 10, 13, 25

Designed by Harald Peter.
Set in Linofilm Palatino, a 20th century
typeface resembling a Venetian, designed
by Hermann Zapf of Frankfurt.
Printed on Hallmark Eggshell Book paper.